# Our Team

## KIMBERLEY DUNN

*The Abbey Editor & Owner of The Admont Library*

Born in Paris, Kimberley has spent the past twenty years living in London, Dallas, Miami, Paris, and Atlanta. From a young age, she has always had a love for books, especially classics. She would all too often look forward to Barnes and Nobles' "Buy 1 Get 1 Free" sale on Classic Starts, abridged classics for children. Currently in Atlanta, Kimberley enjoys collecting and selling antiquarian books, writing poetry, and reading.

## THE ADMONT LIBRARY

*Antiquarian Bookstore & Aspiring Archive*

Inspired by the largest monastic library in the world, The Admont Library aims to capture the unparalleled beauty and baroque aesthetic of Austria's Admont Abbey. While specializing in classics, we sell books of all genres and aim to offer the gift of knowledge with both style and care. Aiming to provide all with an enhanced reading experience, we guarantee that every order includes a complimentary brew + bookmark, decorative packaging, and free shipping.

# Contents

# editor's note

Welcome to The Abbey. Like The Admont Library, our magazine seeks to provide readers with the ultimate reading experience. Here we let creativity, freedom of expression, and a passion for literature run wild.

The Abbey serves as a place for avid readers, scholars, and admirers of classic literature alike in its combination of a love for books with pleasing, medieval-inspired aesthetics. Whether just venturing into the world of collecting rare books or a passionate reader, you'll find The Abbey a place to call home.

*Kimberley dunn*

**BECAUSE READING ISN'T JUST AN EXPERIENCE: IT'S AN ADVENTURE.**

# Cancelling Dostoevsky?

The inherently dangerous discouragement of civil discourse on classical literature remains all but a thing of the past.

Those who daringly venture the realm of controversial literature with the intent of literary and historical criticism confront an all too frequent quagmire of having to dance around potential political incorrectness, the fear of such a transgression ultimately discouraging the discussion - let alone appreciation - of timeless classical works.

Writer Paolo Nori, invited to conduct guest lectures on Dostoevsky at the University of Milano-Bicocca, met considerable frustration upon the Italian University's decision to "postpone the course" in an effort to "avoid any controversy...during a time of strong tensions."  Amidst the current controversies regarding the appreciation of Russian literature, especially with the ongoing invasion of Ukraine, such a well-intentioned act of protest edges dangerously toward the censorship of literature and discouragement of civil discourse.

Known for his invigorating existential works, including *Notes from Underground*, *Crime and Punishment*, and *The Brothers Karamazov*, Dostoevsky has certainly attained his place alongside Leo Tolstoy as one of the greatest writers of all time. Dostoevsky faced the sentencing of death by firing squad in 1849 on the account of reading banned books and taking part in allegedly antigovernment activities associated with a "radical intellectual discussion group," the Petrashevsky Circle. Spared from execution at the last minute, Dostoevsky was sent to a Siberian labor camp, where he remained over the course of four years.

What's rather amusing in all this is that when taken into thought in a modern context, there ironically emerges two distinctive Russian figures that Russia's own president, Vladimir Putin, has to choose from when it comes to that of his favorite authors: Dostoevsky for his exceptionalism versus Tolstoy for his prospect of the universality of all human experience, regardless of one's nationality, culture, or religion.

Even more ironically, each of the writers managed to create what prove some of the most convincing arguments in favor of non-violent resistance to evil in the history of the human race.

And yet given Russia's historic struggle to withstand the influence of Westernization and reinforce a uniform national identity, Putin quite fervidly turns to capitalizing on the nature of Dostoevsky's exceptionalism in the name of justifying his envisioned expansion of the former Russian empire.

Among several of Dostoevsky's works, notes Laura Goering, professor of Russian at Carleton College, "the West is depicted as something seductive, yet soulless, a temptation to be resisted at all costs." Though some of Dostoevsky's concerns with the nihilistic ideals emerging with the Enlightenment are with good reason. With a deep understanding as to the extremes to which man proves capable upon his time in Siberia, Dostoevsky correctly conveys the undeniable value in the understanding of ideologies that have no moral ground.

Repeatedly in Russian literature, Goering emphasizes, "we see a claim to a kind of spiritual and moral exceptionalism that is fundamental to Putin's rhetoric. In the wake of the collapse of the Soviet Union, which Putin called the 'biggest geopolitical catastrophe of the century,' it is not surprising that he continues to draw on the myth of a Russia divinely foreordained to stand firm against the corrupting forces of the West."

Regardless of Dostoevsky's nationalistic sentiments, however, Putin seems to utterly misinterpret and undermine the very essence of Dostoevsky's philosophy, the very which being what comes to position him beside Tolstoy as one of the greatest writers of all time.

As such, to truly understand how Putin so greatly came to miscalculate the world's reaction to his sudden invasion of Ukraine, one merely has to turn to one of Dostoevsky's own characters: Rodion Raskolnikov.

The fact that Dostoevsky himself endured such hardship for expressing his own beliefs, contrary to that of the Russian intelligentsia of the time, calls into question as to what purpose it serves to censure his writing almost two hundred years after his death. Admittedly, Vladimir Putin has been emphatically open about his admiration for both Dostoevsky and Tolstoy.

Though Dostoevsky took part in socialist and liberal literary circles, he radically shifted his political stance after his time in Siberia, which redefined his understanding of Christian salvation and the commonality of man. Renouncing the ideals aligned with utopian socialism, he thereby reinforced that of which promote nationalism and the resurrection of the Russian Orthodox Church.

*"Dostoevsky recognized the grounding essence of religion's moral parameters, which, when examined in terms of values as opposed to dogmatically, give way to favorable outcomes for the future."*

Dostoevsky's nationalism is heavily intertwined with Orthodoxy in that he claimed that in the wake of God's death upon the spread of the European Enlightenment across Russia emerged a moral vacuum, void of the only to be filled by utilitarian ideologies. Dostoevsky recognized the grounding essence of religion's moral parameters, which, when examined in terms of values as opposed to dogmatically, give way to favorable outcomes for the future. His messianic vision takes its form from the idea that Russia was the most spiritually developed of all other nations and thereby destined to unite and lead the others. Contrastingly, Tolstoy firmly believed in each nation's bearing of its own unique traditions, none better nor worse than the others. While a patriot, Tolstoy was certainly not a nationalist and believed in the distinct genius and dignity of each culture.

Inauspiciously, both the fall of the Soviet Union and tumult of 20th century Russian history have propelled Russians to cling toward Dostoevsky's starker, messianic vision over that of Tolstoy's more collective prospect of universal humanity.

Developing the "superman" theory in Crime and Punishment, Dostoevsky follows Raskolnikov, an impoverished student tormented by his own extreme nihilism, and his pursuit of utilitarian ideals, leading him to murder an old woman, a pawnbroker he conceives as "stupid, ailing, greedy...good for nothing." Delving into the unraveling of Raskolnikov's paranoia, fear, and madness in the face of his crime, Dostoevsky demonstrates the danger of drawing away from the grounding essence of religion's moral parameters, one then perceiving himself capable of transcending beyond the boundaries of good and evil in the name of taking on the role of God himself, ultimately making way for anarchic chaos, destruction, and a lack of morality.

Quite similarly to Raskolnikov, Putin finds himself immersed in increased isolation, his own advisors misleading him throughout the course of the war and merely telling what he desires to hear.  Such isolation thereby makes way for Putin to perceive himself as a Napoleon-like figure, or superman, capable of overstepping the bounds of good and evil that otherwise govern all others. Putin becoming overcome with visions of reinforcing the might of the former Russian empire, his seclusion encourages and propels the pursuit of utilitarian ideals in the name of achieving some greater good. All of which to say, therefore, that despite his adoration for Russian literature, Putin's alienation from society displays his ironic unfamiliarity with the ideals which compose the Russian soul.

The symbolic discouragement of celebrating or even examining Russian literature, however, has quite naturally sown itself within the field of collective undergrowth of gestural protest, acclimatizing with the course of current affairs, that germinates amidst Western culture on the account of the ongoing, increasingly inhumane events in Ukraine. The rise of such a movement that seeks to disregard Russian literature and culture, while perhaps good-natured in its endeavor to blatantly announce its granted opposition to Russia's unwarranted offensive, precariously verges toward the constricted nature of a world not unlike that of Fahrenheit 451, void of open discourse, and inherently raises two major concerns: the continual censorship of literature and the dangerous implications of "cancelling" entire cultures.

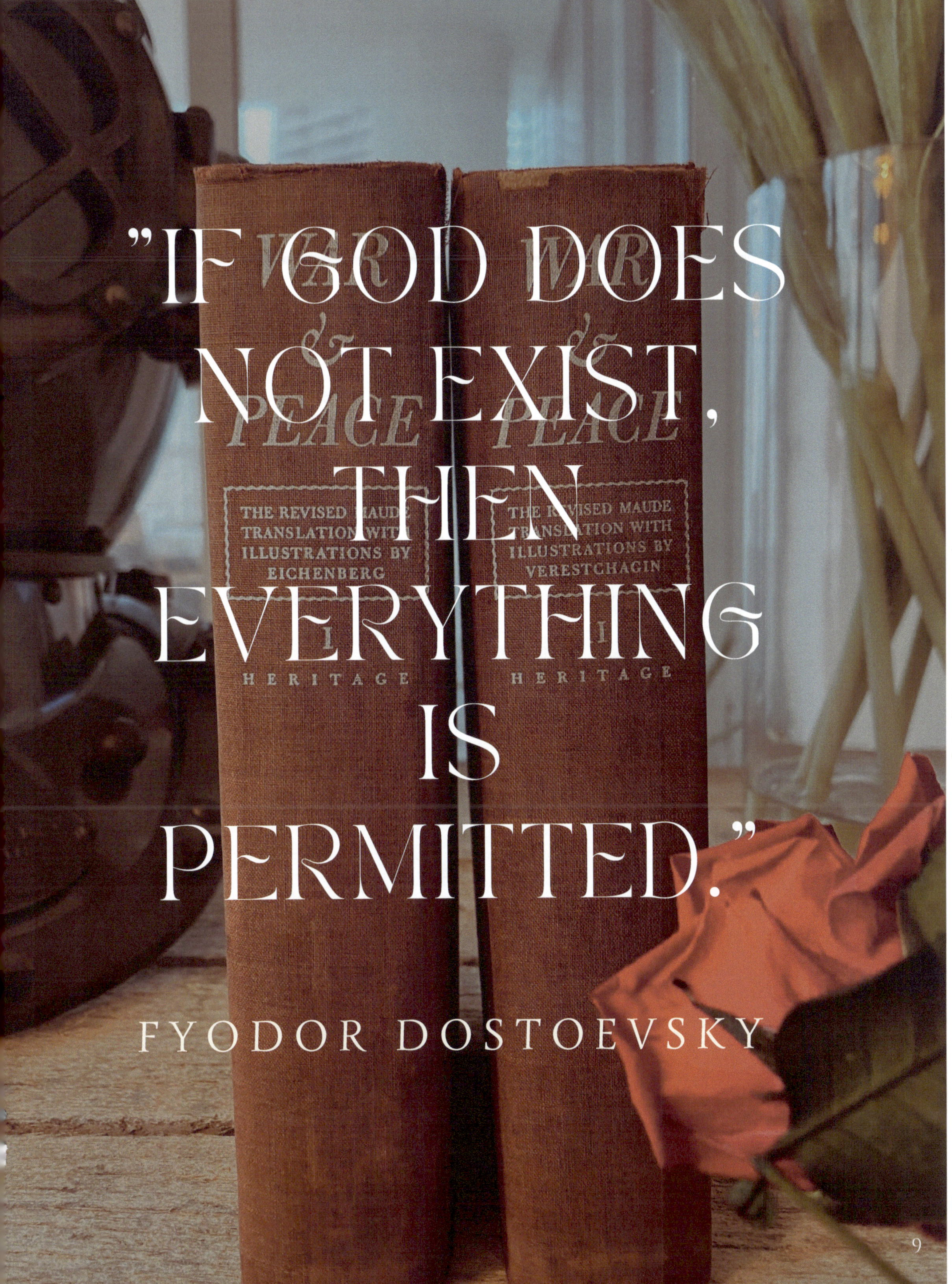

"IF GOD DOES NOT EXIST, THEN EVERYTHING IS PERMITTED."
FYODOR DOSTOEVSKY

# *writing your own*
# SHAKESPEAREAN SONNET

Shakespeare has left a timeless mark on the world through his plays (i.e. *Romeo and Juliet*, *Hamlet*, *Macbeth*), however, historians and those in academia recognize him equivalently for his remarkably touching sonnets. The poetic form of a sonnet originates in Italy, and Shakespeare popularized this manner of poetry after publishing 154 sonnets in 1609 - almost all of which being love poems.  Sonnets vary in terms of their other characteristics, but Shakespeare's sonnets in particular feature the following distinctive attributes:

- 14 lines
- iambic pentameter
- a volta (shift in mood) in between the second and third stanzas
- three quatrains (ABAB rhyme scheme)
- final couplet - usually unexpected or including a sudden twist
- covering themes such as sorrow, love, and desperation

With time, sonnets have quite naturally lost their popularity amongst modern-day writers and laid to rest. Nevertheless, I encourage you to follow the guidelines above and attempt at writing a sonnet of your own. Let us engage in the revival of the Shakespearean sonnet!

A poet myself,  I have found a burgeoning gladness in writing sonnets - especially ones that explore atypical themes or ones that one wouldn't expect from these poems. There is something indescribable that appears to make itself known in one's heart with the completion of such an art. Naturally, I have provided one of my own works and sincerely hope you find enjoyment in what I consider a favorite of mine.

# a fitful sleep

art thou soft, tell-tale heart that speaks to me?
for you shall never know how much i care.
as your supple skin ceases not to please -
neither do your tendrils of blooming hair.

please me as you know how, my dear temptress.
*rejoice!* graceful as the bellowing wind,
i have become one with you, so senseless.
take me into the earth for i have sinned.

melancholy drivel i call it, *love.*
the mutterings of a *madman* i'd say!
where have you gone since i last saw you, *dove?*
feverish dreams are not that fit to stay.

i smell the ochre in my very bones,
i burn to death as do ancient tomes.

# Modern Literary Censorship

Literary censorship hardly constitutes as a new or dying practice, and the continuance of which, particularly toward classical works, such as 1984, Fahrenheit 451, Animal Farm, and Brave New World, whose contents contain valuable life lessons that pertain to the thrum of modern society, hinders generational understanding of the importance of literature.

Such censorship makes itself known not merely through banning books but the discouragement of discussions that while may prove controversial or polarizing are valuable in their ability to unveil issues that are uniquely capable of being developed through the art of the written and oratory word.

There is an understandable hesitation, for instance, with regard to the perfect timing of when to begin incorporating books featuring mature contents into a school curriculum, however, for many, literature serves as the very exposure that propels youth into adulthood. The fine line, however, lies in that high level high school classes such as AP Literature & Composition expect a seriousness of students that enables them to examine mature, real-world themes from a critical and analytic perspective. Moreover, school administrators and those seeking to censor classic literature for their inclusion of uncomfortable historical topics quite often hide behind the excuse of maturity rather than flat out declaring their opposition to the discussion of books' themes.

The implicative danger of cancel culture and censorship has shown itself most recently with the removal of the book *Maus* from an eighth-grade curriculum in McMinn County, Tennessee on the account of the book's "rough, objectionable language." The author of *Maus*, Art Spiegelman, said he was positively baffled by the decision. "This is disturbing imagery," he said in an interview on Holocaust Remembrance Day. "But you know what? It's disturbing history."

The celebration of "banned" books serves its purpose in providing an unfiltered lens on complex and ever-relevant issues. Even when reading "outdated" works filled with biases, prejudice, as so forth. it is by understanding the formulation of such view points that one can then pinpoint their fatal flaws that similarly fuel prejudicial thinking today. It is necessary to examine the mistakes of history and the past so as not to repeat them but rather advance with a learned lens. To avoid exposure to the past is to avoid confronting the innate and unavoidable flaws of human nature that have to be understood to move forward. With a deeper understanding of history, the youth of today gain the opportunity to hone and develop their own views, free of the politicized path that governs modern journalism.

So why books of all things? Why ban the prototype of what stands for intellectual advancement? Why not direct efforts toward addressing the more pressing concerns that shape the youth of today and threaten the very making of their morality? These here are questions to consider amongst ourselves but also to those opposing the fundamental right of civil discourse and literary critical analysis, regardless of a book's "trying" contents.

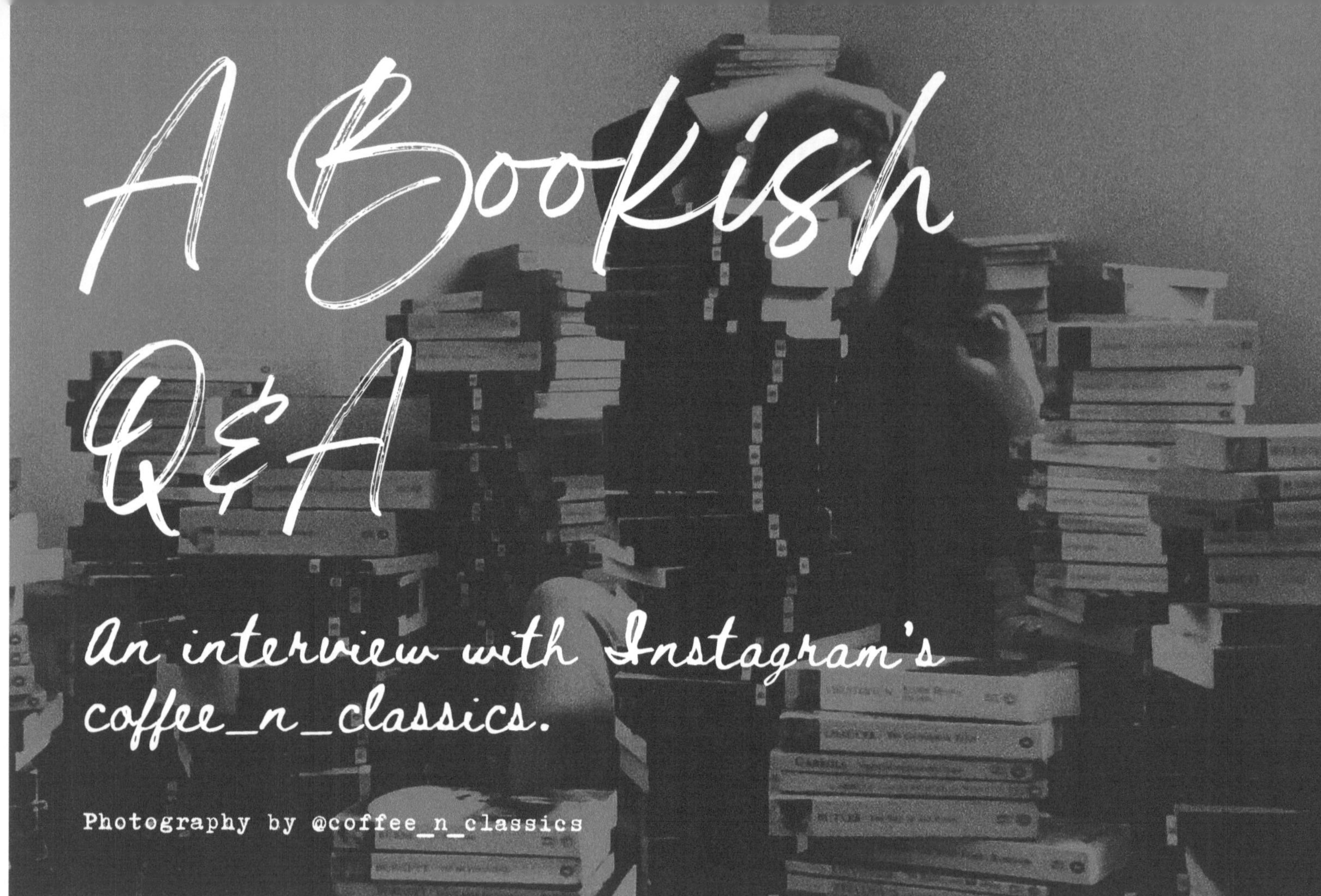




## Tell us about yourself.

I am Antonia, a lady in her 20's. I lived in Metro Manila, Philippines and I am a licensed architect with a passion for painting, reading classic books, and having a boundless love for coffee and tea. I love anything about vintage things, especially in terms of fashion and cameras. A hobby of mine that I can't and will never let go of is journaling and sticking ephemera in my journals because I'm a sentimental person and mostly, it is those little things that matter to me.

## Who is your favorite writer? What's something they've written that particularly resonates with you?

With his way of writing, aside from Jane Austen which I also most adore dearly, Oscar Wilde is my current favorite writer, and his creation entitled, "Only Dull People Are Brilliant at Breakfast" is something that I most resonate with because of the way he defines something in it and then self argues with it until it becomes a statement like how I sometimes observe something on my daily basis, weigh things about it, and then create a theory of it.

## What inspired your passion for books and/or reading?

My answer to this question every time it is asked will never change and the inspiration behind my passion for books and/or reading is my family; which started with my mother who bought and patiently read bedtime stories with me as I requested to repeat them over and over again when I was a kid; then to my late aunt who had a wide collection of romantic novels and whom I have become fascinated to Encyclopedias with for she was selling sets of those before; to my late grandfather who quietly enjoyed reading thriller and suspense novels while also having shelves full of hardbound books of Reader's Digest that are all about golf, his favorite sport; and to my other late aunt who opened me to another level of reading with visuals at a young age through her many collections of Archie comics and other local comics which became my past time especially summer breaks at the age of six.

## What is your favorite classic and why?

My favorite classics of all time are "Alice's Adventures in Wonderland" and "Through the Looking Glass" by Lewis Carroll for these are my comfort and companion every time I was feeling that I don't belong in something or in somewhere. With the help of these creations of him, I let it in myself sink in that I can be my own whimsically and majestically weird wonderland. That I don't have to shape myself and fit into something or somewhere that I am not.

**What's on your wish-list? What rare find are you searching for or just wish you had?**

My wish list is full of books in Penguin Classics black spine edition that I still haven't owned. I know that the collection in this edition is like an endless case but sometimes, I dream of owning a library full of classics in this edition.

**What's your most prized possession (book-related or otherwise)?**

My most prized possessions are the only remaining fictional book of my late grandfather entitled, "Independence Day" from the screenplay and novelization by Dean Devlin & Roland Emmerich and Stephen Molstad, and his vintage film camera that is displayed together with my shelf of vintage camera collections.

**What are you currently reading?**

Right now, I'm currently continuing Fyodor Dostoyevsky's "The Brothers Karamazov" while also started reading "Letters from a Stoic" by Seneca again.

**What's your favorite opening line from a novel?**

My favorite opening line from a novel is from Jane Austen's Pride and Prejudice which says, "It is a truth universally acknowledged, that a single man in possession of a good fortune, must be in want of a wife" for it portrays how significant a woman's role in the world of man.

**Who is your all-time favorite character and why?**

Along with my favorite classic from the previous question, my all-time favorite character is and will always be Alice from Lewis Carroll's "Alice's Adventures in Wonderland" and "Through the Looking Glass" because this character gave life to my soul that craves an escape from reality at times when life is giving us more lemons than we can handle.

**Where do you keep your books?**

My books stay in my room for I know that it's the safest place for them and I always want them all to be nearest in my sight. They're one of my sources of inspiration—looking at them on my bookshelves.

Locally speaking, my all-time favorite bookstores are "Fully Booked" and "Booksale." Internationally speaking though I haven't been to it, ever since I have known it is the "Shakespeare and Company" bookstore in Paris, France for in my research, it holds a lot of historic moments in the world of literature.



When talking about the outdoors, a favorite place of mine to read are corner seats of cafes or seats anywhere near the walls of cafes so I can feel a division of privacy while enjoying the whole environment and circulation of the cafe. Another is libraries if I tend to search for a more focused and quiet time for reading. If in terms of inside the house, my favorite place to read will always be my room.

My favorite memory of the library particularly our university library during my college days is when the guards and library assistants already greet me as their close friends for I am always hanging out for hours and hours in there, especially during the long break hours and mostly reaches the maximum number of books allowed in borrowing.

**Who's your favorite antagonist and why?**

My current favorite antagonist is Mr. Edward Hyde from Robert Louis Stevenson's "The Strange Case of Dr. Jekyll and Mr. Hyde" for not only he's both the protagonist and antagonist but he, the antagonist himself is battling the villain or evil within him which was brilliantly created and played by Stevenson. That Mr. Hyde himself is aware of how uncontrollable his demons are and wanted to ask for help but at the same time, thirstily craves the people who wanted to save him from his madness.

**What book character reminds you of yourself?**

A book character that dearly and closely reminds me of myself is Griet from "Girl With A Pearl Earring" by Tracy Chevalier for I resonate with how she deeply observes every art material that Vermeer uses in his studio and how she passionately wanted to also learn the process of making the different pigments of the paint he uses. It's the enthusiasm for the world of art most especially painting that I deeply resonate with Griet.

**What are you most looking forward to this year?**

As practical as everything is and due to the evolving phase of the world, all I am ever and always looking forward and praying to this year is the continued good health and safety of my family and loved ones.

# Women in
# The Rare Book Trade

**Exploring the role of women in the industry with Susan Benne, Executive Director of the Antiquarian Bookseller's Association of America.**

Consider the rare book industry for a moment. Who comes to mind? You likely picture a middle-aged to older man with a greying beard and whiskers, glasses perched on the edge of his nose, reading and collecting first editions. Surrounding him are books, piled about in tilting stacks - books written by… well, *even more* middle-aged to older men.

In taking a look at today's rare book industry, it is without a question more diverse than say even fifteen years ago, women-owned bookstores now being increasingly on the rise; however, this has not always been the case; not to mention, there is still much room for the continual development of inclusivity in the bookselling trade.

The question, therefore, is not only how the rare book business has progressed to where it is today but also what it means to be a woman (in a male-dominated industry), navigating trials and tribulations that emerge as one takes part in the invigorating endeavor of collecting and selling antiquarian and 'rare' books.

# A Brief History of Rare Bookselling

Collecting and selling rare books is a practice that dates back to the Middle Ages, however, the enterprise truly came into prominence during the 18th and 19th centuries. Monasteries, scholars, and the wealthy have - for quite some time - sought to conserve books, illuminated manuscripts, religious texts, and the like. Most of the early booksellers and collectors were affluent Dukes or aristocrats, given women's limited access to education or the financial means to start a bookstore in the first place.

Something that most people might not know, however, is that throughout the Middle Ages, it wasn't only monks who served as scribes, producing and preserving illuminated manuscripts - nuns too, were literate. Consider Ende, the first known female illuminator of Spain or perhaps the bestselling medieval poet, Christine de Pizan - or even Amat-Mamu, a Mesopotamian priestess and temple scribe - all of which display the fact that female scribes have existed across history.

Subsequently, not only do we skim over the fact that female scribes and writers were indeed at the forefront of intellectual advancements during and after the Middle Ages, but what remains unmentioned - as we return back to the subject of the rare book trade - is the role they served alongside monks in preserving the very texts they produced. This then quite naturally leads us to the official rise of what we now consider the 'modern' antiquarian and rare bookselling industry.

With the fight for equal opportunity and women's rights taking off in the 19th century, women's literacy rates grew, meaning the emergence of female librarians, booksellers, and archivists. During this period, women  began inheriting printing presses or bookstores from their male relatives. This then quite naturally brings us to the development of what we now consider the 'modern' antiquarian bookselling industry.

As the Antiquarian Association of America so rightly asserts (*abaa.org*), it was the prominence of the printing press in the United States in the 1800s that led to the establishment of the modern rare book trade. Books were made more widely available and as time passed, they began to appeal to a larger audience. With a rise in literacy rates among women, the once faraway aspiration of female booksellers actually became a reality. Women finally began to occupy a space in the world of bookselling.

Take Ann Lemoine, for instance, the first fully-independent female chapbook publisher in all of England. Working during the late 18th century, she contributed to the increasing prominence of chapbooks and pamphlets, making literature more common and affordable. This shift from exclusivity to accessibility was essential in the development of the modern antiquarian book trade, in which women would then take on leading roles.

# SUSAN
## Benne

# ABAA
## Executive Director

As the abolitionist and suffragette movements became more pronounced, bookshops run by women in the 19th century  doubled, serving as spaces for intellectual exchange and social activism.

And with the arrival of the 20th century, women like Madeleine B. Stern became renowned antiquarian booksellers and bibliographers. The rare book trade's professionalization saw women at the forefront. By the mid-20th century, women were active in organizations such as Antiquarian Bookselling Association of America and the International League of Antiquarian Booksellers (ILAB), promoting ethical standards within the trade.

Today, women-owned rare bookstores are thriving, with many female booksellers using social media to attract customers. Initiatives like The Honey & Wax Book Collecting Prize, founded by Heather O'Donnell, celebrate young female book collectors and even encourage future generations to participate in the trade.

The question still remains, however, what exactly does being a woman in the rare book industry in this day and age involve? To answer that question is Susan Benne.

The current Executive Director of the Antiquarian Booksellers' Association of America (ABAA), Susan Benne, brings a unique background to her role, which she has held for several years now. Her path to overseeing the most prestigious association of antiquarian booksellers in the U.S. is marked by an unexpected journey from the world of performing arts into rare books, blending creativity with management expertise.

Transitioning to the rare book industry occurred after being offered a job by rare book Susan specializing in children's and illustrated books. She reminisces, "I was actually dating a guy whose parents were rare book dealers...and they had always needed somebody to hire ... they said, are you interested in doing this? We know you're not super happy in your existing job outside of college, but would you like to work for us? And I was like, yeah, absolutely!"

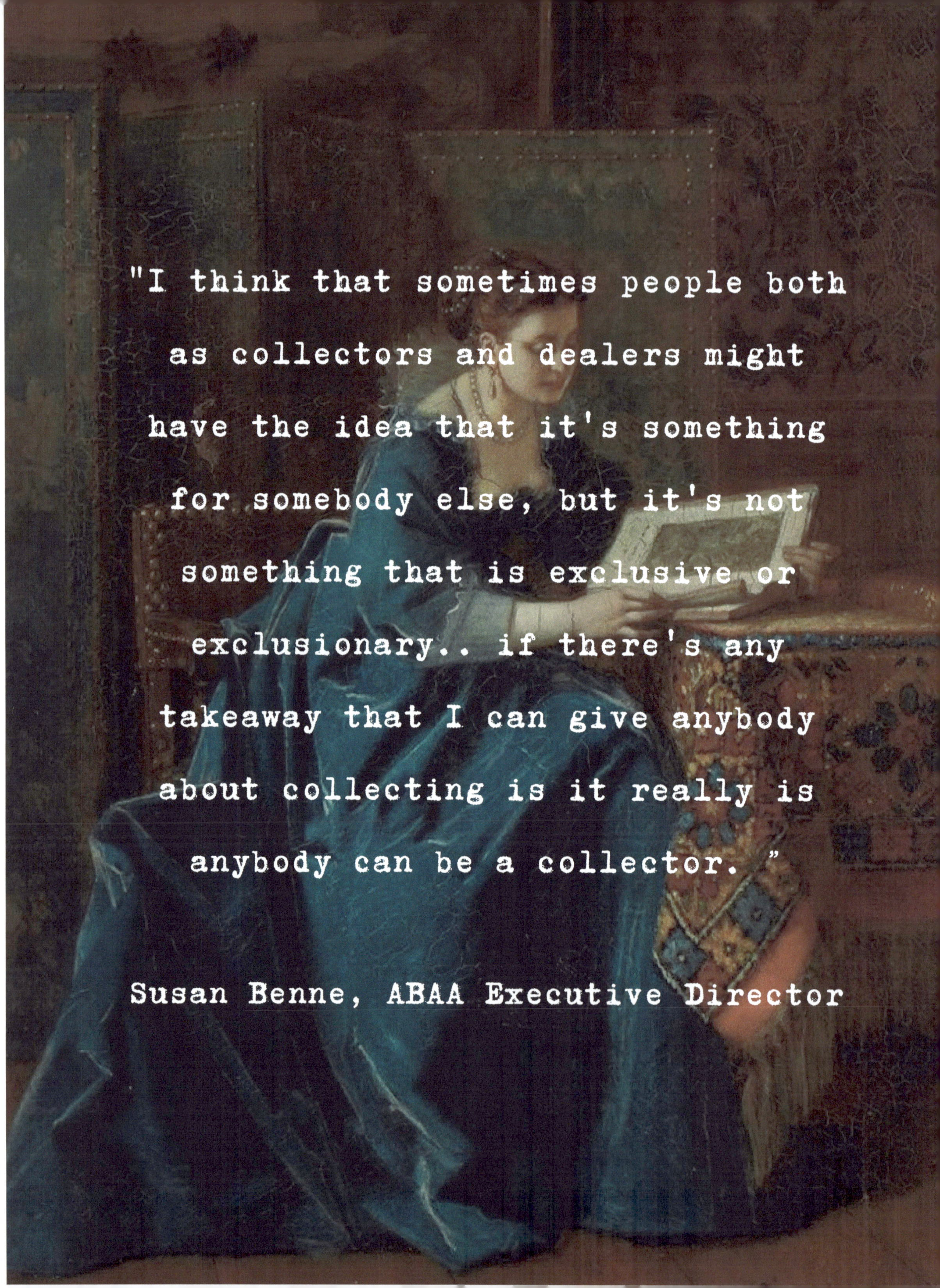

"I think that sometimes people both
as collectors and dealers might
have the idea that it's something
for somebody else, but it's not
something that is exclusive or
exclusionary.. if there's any
takeaway that I can give anybody
about collecting is it really is
anybody can be a collector. "

Susan Benne, ABAA Executive Director

Susan Benne's journey to becoming the Executive Director of the ABAA has been marked by an eclectic background and unique transitions. She began in the world of high-paced arts management in Manhattan, working with a prominent opera singer—a world far removed from her later work cataloging books, such as those on the whimsical topic of mermaids. Her transition into the antiquarian book trade set the foundation for a future where she would work alongside major figures in the field, including the head of the New York Antiquarian Book Fair.

Reflecting on her familiarity with the ABAA even before her directorship, Susan notes, "I knew about the ABAA and its importance, its ethics, the type of people that it attracted to become members. I had certainly been to the New York Book Fair before." Stepping into the role, however, broadened her perspective: "Once I started directing, it really opened my eyes to the different types of materials that individuals sell and collect outside of the realm of children's and illustrated," she explains. Susan found herself working closely with international dealers, an opportunity that enriched her understanding of the global reach of the trade. When the ABAA announced the search for a new director, she eagerly applied, driven by a love for her work and a commitment to advancing the organization.

There isn't exactly a guidebook out there on how to become Director of the ABAA, given the career occupies its own niche. On that note, Susan observes, "As you can imagine, it's kind of an unusual [career path]...you can't really go to school for it." Her combined experience working for both a dealer and the New York Antiquarian Book Fair organizer positioned her well for the job. This blend of roles facilitated a smooth transition, as she already "knew a lot of the players" in the field. Twenty years later, Susan continues to contribute to growing the ABAA, expanding its programs and strengthening its visibility within the antiquarian book community and beyond.

Susan Benne's perspective on collecting is one of inclusivity and accessibility, aiming to demystify the antiquarian book trade. She challenges the perception that collecting rare books or materials is only for the wealthy or the elite. "If there's any takeaway that I can give anybody about collecting," she emphasizes, "it really is anybody can be a collector." For her, the act of collecting is not defined by large budgets but by personal interest and passion. Susan encourages collectors to "make your own topic...spend as much or as little as you want," underscoring that collections can start with a single meaningful item and evolve from there. Whether it's rare scientific materials or something unique to the collector, the value lies in personal resonance rather than monetary worth.

In conclusion, Susan Benne's dedication to inclusivity extends beyond the accessibility of collecting; it reflects a broader commitment to building a supportive community within the antiquarian book trade. She highlights that many dealers are eager to share their insights, recognizing that they, too, began as newcomers. "There are a lot of people who are so happy to impart their knowledge," she remarks, noting that they share a common experience in starting out. This welcoming spirit is bolstered by programs such as the Colorado Antiquarian Book Seminar and rare book schools in Los Angeles and at UVA, though such formal avenues remain relatively few.

As we return to the topic in question as a whole - the presence of women in the rare book industry has steadily increased, reshaping what was once a largely male-dominated field. Pioneers like Susan Benne exemplify the impact of women who bring diverse perspectives and an emphasis on inclusivity and accessibility. Through her work with the Antiquarian Booksellers' Association of America (ABAA), Susan has highlighted the need to break down barriers to entry, encouraging not only diverse collections but also a welcoming environment for new collectors and dealers of all backgrounds.

Women like Susan have influenced the trade not only by championing ethical standards and community building but also by creating pathways for mentorship and knowledge-sharing. This has been essential for widening access to the antiquarian world, ensuring that rare book collecting and dealing are perceived as attainable for everyone. By advancing a culture of support, Susan and other women leaders have strengthened the rare book community, leaving an indelible mark on its future.

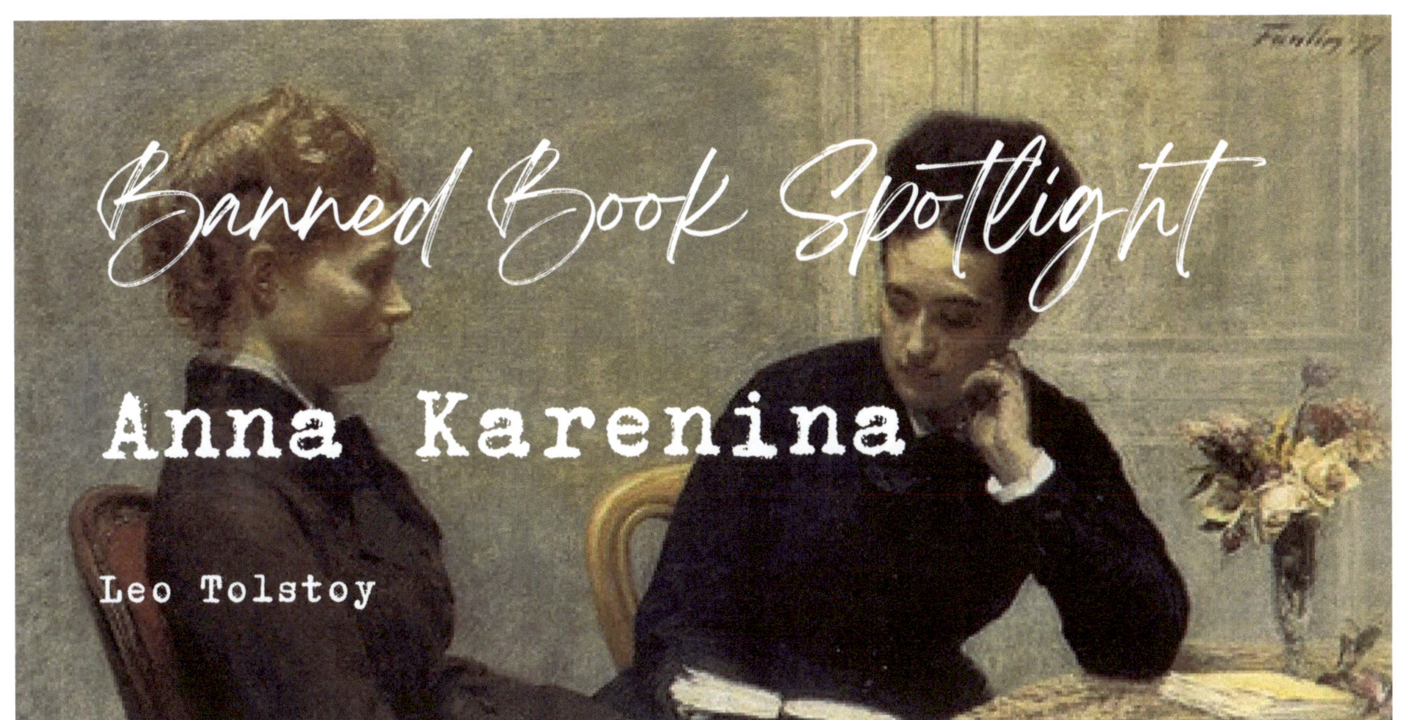

# Banned Book Spotlight
# Anna Karenina

Leo Tolstoy

When one thinks of banned books, *Anna Karenina* is all but the first one that comes to mind. The novel follows the love affair of a married woman and member of high society, Anna, who finds herself having to flee with her lover, Count Vronsky. The book easily stands as one of the greatest of all time. Nevertheless, the treasure of a novel was among those banned in Florida within the last year, alongside Hemingway's *For Whom the Bell Tolls* and Toni Morrison's *The Bluest Eye*.

A report released in April by *Pen America,* a non-profit advocating for free speech, Florida had 3,135 book bans recorded from July 2021 to December 2023 - the highest in the country.

There is quite the irony in this, for Florida, as a state, houses people with more conservative views - people who fully embrace what America stands for. And so, the very people who should be aligned with intellectual freedom within education are against it. In other words, frantic conservative parents are opposing the content of more "controversial" literature with the argument that the contents of the books in question are inappropriate. Tolstoy would differ - and so do those who strive to have the freedom to read what they wish and expose themselves to the truths that can be found within great works of literature.

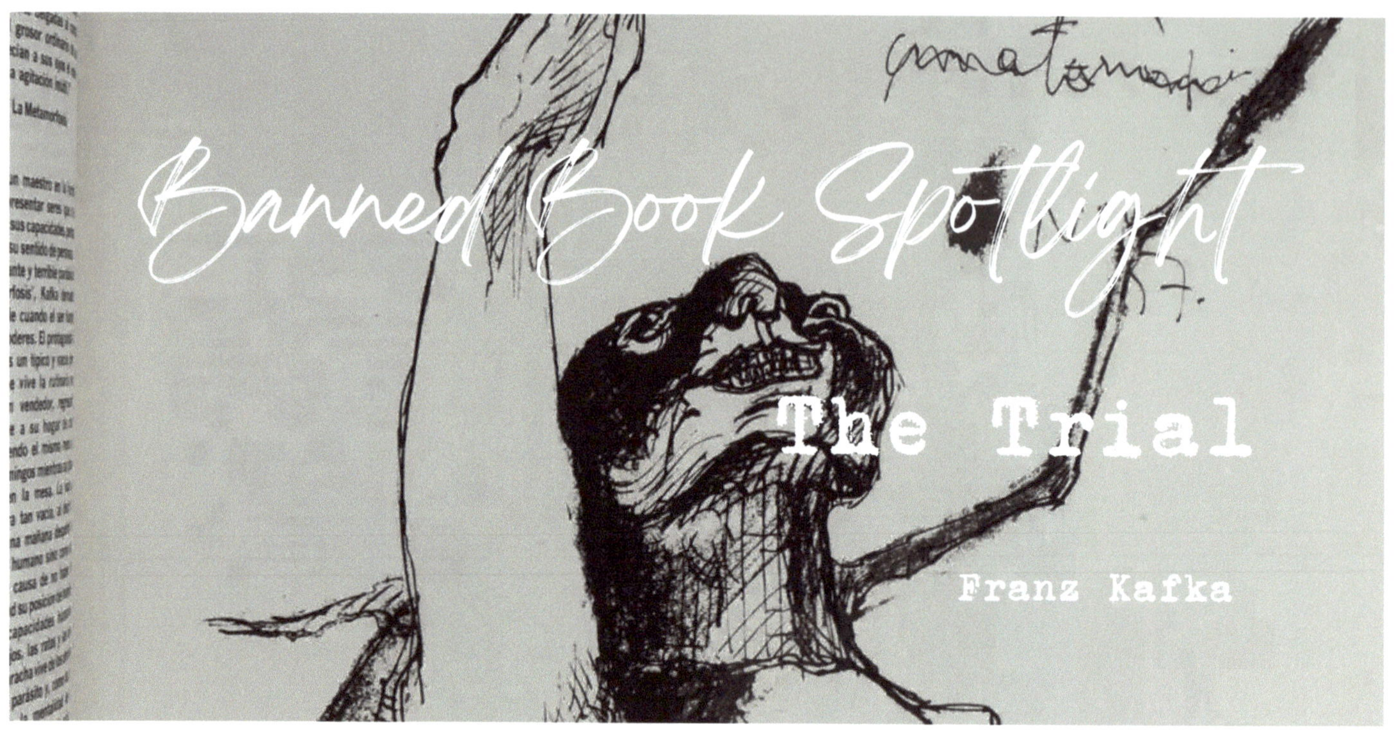

Franz Kafka, one of the most prolific writers of the 20th century, is known for his works *The Trial, Metamorphosis, The Castle,* and *Amerika.* Kafka's *The Trial* follows Josef K, who finds himself on trial for a crime he supposedly commit, the details of which he is all but privy to.

Kafka's home of Czechoslovakia banned his writings while the region was under Nazi occupation during World War II. After the war, the Soviet regime which governed Czechoslovakia still deemed Kafka's *The Trial* with suspicion, dubbing Kafka's work as "decadent and defeatist."

Given that Kafka wrote his novels in German, a language which Czechs have looked down upon after the war, inhabitants of Kafka's native city of Prague - for quite some time - didn't consider his work as having derived from one of their own.

The backlash with which Kafka's *The Trial* has been met is not a surprise, though, for any novel that would discuss the dangers of totalitarian regimes and harsh realities of living in bureaucracies in such a way would likely face prohibition from the perpetrators themselves. Always, however, has Kafka's work deserved to be appreciation for its ability to capture the absurdity of lifle as well as its unspoken truths.

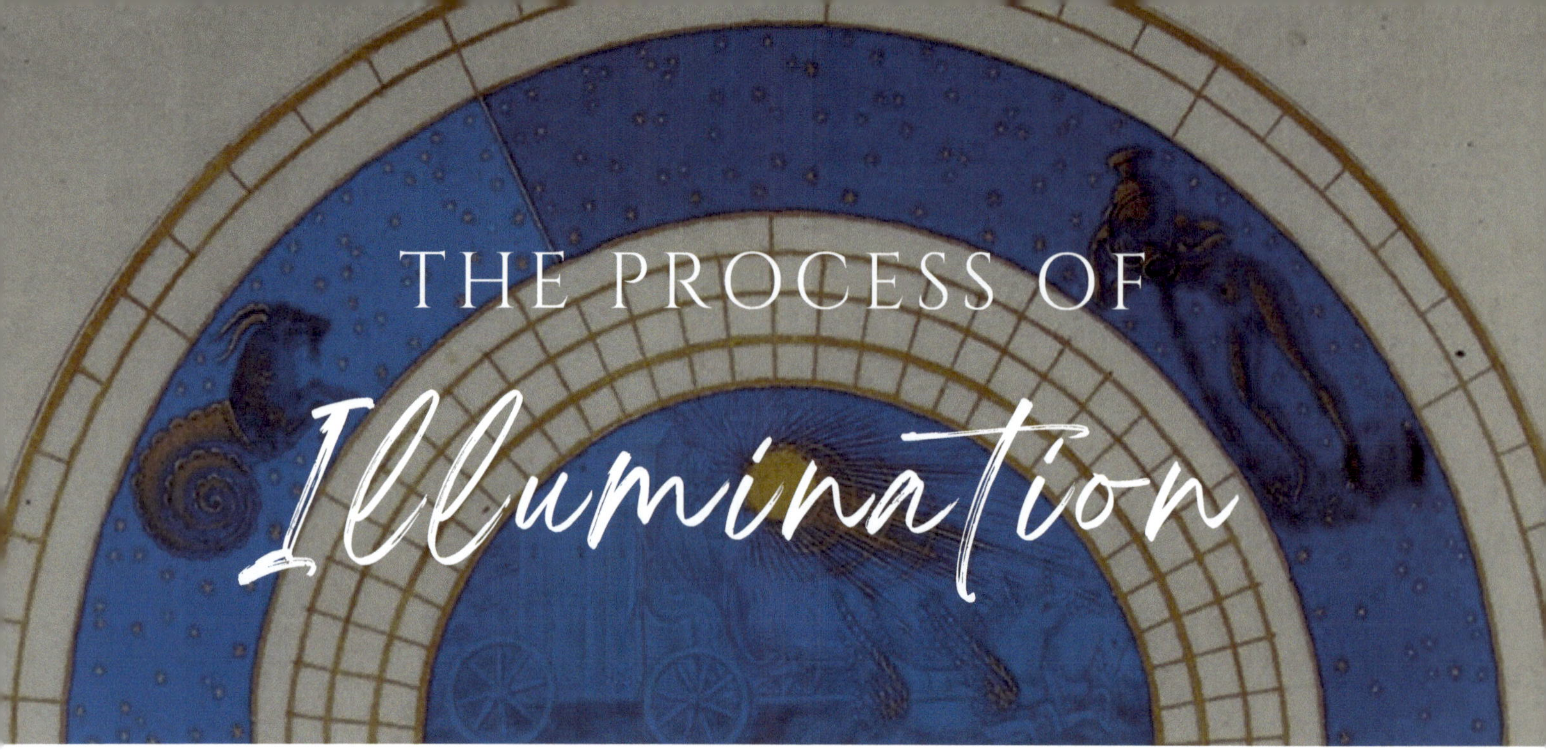

# THE PROCESS OF
# *Illumination*

## Materials:

- Tracing Paper (optional)
- Hot Pressed Watercolor Paper
- Tempera or Gouache Paint
- Pencil (Fineliner pens - optional)
- Paintbrushes
- A metal leaf adhesive (e.g. liquid gesso, gum ammoniac, or a general gilding adhesive)
- Burnisher (e.g. bone folder, agate stone)
- Gold leaf or watercolour
- Precut Goose quills (optional)
- Iron Gall Ink (optional)

## Choosing your Medium

Medieval manuscripts were traditionally written on parchment or vellum (calfskin). The terms are oftentimes interchangeable, however, "parchment" refers to any animal skin once it has been prepared for writing whereas "vellum" explicitly derives from calfskin.

The preparation of parchment is an arduous process, in which the skin is soaked in lime water, stretched across a frame, and scraped to remove any remaining hair. When properly prepared, however, parchment far surpasses any paper as a writing medium in both its longevity and unusual working properties, creating a raised bed upon coming into contact with the paint.

Regardless of one's skill level as an artist, watercolor paper serves as far more of an accessible and affordable alternative to parchment, at least until one has become familiar with the process of making a manuscript.

# Scribery

Often overlooked, quills are actually the most basic and essential component of producing any manuscript. In fact, they often serve as the symbol of the scribal trade. Medieval quills were traditionally taken from the first five flight feathers of large-feathered birds (often geese or swans) and were then stripped down until solely the shaft remained. Scribes then used a penknife to cut and sharpen their quills; the knife could also be used to scrape away any mistakes.

For advanced scribes looking to take a more traditional route, acquiring a goose quill would be well worth it. As some collect plumage when birds molt, affordable feathers can be found at various craft stores and online marketplaces.

Upon acquiring a suitable quill comes the selection of pigmentation in a form of none other than iron gall ink. The standard for writing ink from the 5th - 19th Centuries, iron gall ink is a permanent blue-black extracted from the tannic acids and iron salts of gall, a growth off of oak trees. Iron gall ink gained its notoriety given that when exposed to air, it soaks well into the parchment as opposed to carbon inks which rub off easily. Well-prepared iron gall inks can be found at various craft stores.

# All That Glitters is Gold

Before painting the manuscript's outline comes one of the most enticing aspects of creating an illuminated manuscript: the gilding of gold leaf. A practice tracing from as early as 400 AD, the application of gold or silver leaf to manuscripts ultimately rose in popularity in tandem with the artistic exploration and technological advancements of the Middle Ages and Renaissance. Accompanied by ornamental gold, the manuscripts' 'illuminating' miniatures foster an understanding of the text, the gold's 'enlightening' luminosity captures captures the movement of daily medieval life.

AMERICA
MARE
PACIFICUM
DEL

MEMENTO
MORI.

To the Reader:

Leunclaviuss
APOLOGY
FOR
ZOSIMUS.
Against the unjust
Reflection
of
Eogrius.
Nicephorus.
Cedrenus.
and others.

Leuncla

HÆC MEA
VOLUP.
TAS.

D. ANTONIUS VANDYCK EQVES
CAROLI REGIS MAGN. C. BRITANANTIUM
ANTVERP.

Regardless of varying gilding techniques, the traditional order of 'illumination' comes in three steps: applying an adhesive, laying metal leaf, and burnishing.

Traditional gilders go about mixing their own liquid gesso, a blend of Plaster of Paris and glue. In substitution of undertaking such an intricate process when exploring the art of illumination, one can use pre-prepared gesso or simple metal leaf adhesive to achieve similar results.

The application of the an adhesive to the manuscript involves the application and burnishing of gold leaf over the desired site of illumination; the leaf is polished once dry with a burnishing tool  such as agate stone or a bone folder. The goal of the burnishing process is to acquire a surface characteristic of a smooth, metallic shine.

An valuable tip to note is that one should apply the adhesive delicately with a thin brush before painting so as to avoid the risk of smudging surrounding work.

## Painting With A Twist

A manuscript's "illumination" stems not only from its characteristic gilded gold but equally from its vividly colored illustrations. Egg tempera was a widely used painting medium throughout the Middle Ages, as well as paints made from glair (beaten egg white) and gum arabic (watercolor).

For those seeking a more accessible route, gouache paint is an equally suitable alternative. Gouache was traditionally used in European illuminated manuscripts as well as Persian miniatures. A pigment consisting of gum arabic and white, gouache is a water-based paint, similar in composition to that of watercolor but modified to make it more opaque. Not to mention, gouache is *rewattable* and *reworkable* in a manner quite unlike other mediums; in being water-soluble, it can be reactivated with a mere drop or two of water even after the paint has dried. And that's it - you're finished!

# Scriveners Disassemble?

Though a popular art between the 13th and 16th centuries, manuscript illumination naturally subsided with the invention of Gutenburg's printing press (c. 1440), propelling a rapid decline in the production of illuminated manuscripts. The literary world shifting toward the pragmatic practice of hand-binding books writing and painting them by hand, illuminated manuscripts became a splendor even further reserved for the wealthy toward the early sixteenth century.

Regardless, illuminated manuscripts remain treasured in their being the most common surviving items of Middle Ages and particular role in carrying forth the transmission of ideas through such illustrative means. The art of manuscript illumination hardly ends with the culmination of its practicality. In fact, the relevance of which still pertains to today in exploring the very development of art and literature. And as a manuscript truly comes to life with the incorporation of gold leaf, its luminosity similarly radiates the celebration of knowledge. The process of manuscript illumination thereby offers to modern scribes, fellow beginners, and those simply intrigued by the illumination process a glimpse into the motions and limitations of the past as well as the similarly impressive illustrations that skillfully bring words to life.